EASY WAYS
WITH

DRIED
FLOWERS

EASY WAYS
WITH
DRIED
FLOWERS

AMELIA
SAINT GEORGE

TIGER BOOKS INTERNATIONAL
LONDON

To Alex

This edition published in 1994 by
Tiger Books International PLC, Twickenham

First published in Great Britain in 1992 by Anaya Publishers Ltd
Strode House, 44–50 Osnaburgh Street, London NW1 3ND
Reprinted 1993

Editor	Coral Walker
Art Director	Jane Forster
Photography	Patrice de Villiers
Design Assistant	Sarah Willis
Painted Backgrounds	Kathy Fillion Richie
Illustration	Kevin Hart

ISBN 1–85501–508–0

Typeset by Bookworm Typesetting, Manchester
Colour reproduction by J. Film Process, Bangkok
Printed and bound in Hong Kong

Contents

Introduction

The wonderful variety of colours, tones, textures and shapes dried flowers offer is truly inspirational. Yet the most exciting displays can be created using the simplest of techniques.

In this book, I have endeavoured to reveal some of the mysteries of dried flower style and inspire those interested in this pastime to attempt really ambitious projects and achieve the most spectacular results with ease.

Dried flowers are extraordinarily flexible, with few of the constraints of their fresh counterparts. For this reason, they can be treated in a completely different way. You can hang them upside down, weave them in your hair, or tie them around parcels.

Each display in this book, whether grand or humble, is beautifully photographed and clearly explained. Where necessary, illustrations are provided to help you understand a more intricate technique.

However, my approach is often a little unorthodox, and I encourage cheating where possible! Glue and sticky tape are great allies and make assembling materials considerably easier.

I have also encouraged gathering your own materials for preservation. Country walks, visits to the beach, windfalls from city parks, or even your own garden can be a rich source of material. Wherever you live there is always some treat to be gathered and saved for later.

It is also challenging and fun to experiment. Do not be restricted to traditional materials. I have used eggs, fungii, nuts, bread, beads, natural burr and bramble, herbs and spices as well as more popular ingredients. You can add to the list: shells, stones, driftwood, seeds and berries, just for example.

I have also explained various techniques for drying and preserving flowers based upon my own experience and mistakes! Do not be daunted by the prospect that this is a highly scientific process, as often the simplest way to dry most flowers is to tie them in bunches and hang them upside down in your spare room!

I hope this book will stimulate your imagination and act as an inspirational tool. I also hope you will be encouraged to copy, adapt or move on further and create your own unique displays.

PLANTING IN ROWS

One wonderful advantage of dried
floral material is its ability to
become virtually an abstract art
form in its own right, enabling
those with a keen eye to exploit this
for visual excitement.

In this chapter I have looked at
using the keener angles of various
floral materials: the upright stems,
the sharp edges of cut spices and
herbs, or even the straight lines of
the container, and exploiting these
to the full. All use rows of
similarly-sized materials, planted in
military precision.

I have created both the avant garde
and the more traditional using this
technique. I think you will agree
that the effects of these displays is
stunning; yet the skills to create
them is minimal. Use the ideas on
the following pages to inspire you to
try others.

Rose baskets

The radiant beauty and vibrant colours of the rose, when in the fullness of life, give way to more subtle tones and textures when dried. Compact buds and blooms; fat, burgeoning rose hips; fragrant petals evoking the bouquet of summer days for winter nights – at every stage in its development, the delightful rose is a perfect choice for preservation.

Dried roses are easy to arrange, providing the display is well-structured, and planting in rows or clusters is an ideal starting point.

With these three rose designs, the Lavender Basket and the Herb and Spice garden later in this chapter, you will be able to combine orderly precision with charm and style.

TALL STANDING ROSES

Gather together 60–80 beautiful roses – I have used 'Gerdo' – and a plain, round basket for the simplest of all arrangements. Have to hand floral foam, thread and sharp scissors. Wide gauzy, chiffon ribbon in two pastel shades will complete the display.

Begin by cutting a piece of floral foam to fit snugly inside your basket. Sort your roses into two piles: one with straight stems and the other with curved stems. Strip off any damaged leaves.

To retain a flat, tailored look to the roses, elevate your arrangement to eye level. When possible, I sit while arranging, so put my basket on several large books or telephone directories.

Take one curved-stemmed rose and plant it into the centre of the foam. This will govern the height of your arrangement, so check that none of your remaining roses is too short. You may need to trim the original.

Each rose will need to stand to the same height, so you may need to trim some stems, as you work.

Place the next rose against the first, always applying pressure to the base of the stem when inserting it into the foam. (Never push from the bud end or the stem might snap.)

Continue using your curved-stemmed roses, planting evenly from the centre outwards. Strip off undamaged leaves as you go, so the arrangement does not become too bulky. These pieces of foliage can be used later to fill in any gaps.

Having used all your curved-stemmed roses, continue working outwards to the edge of the basket using the straight-stemmed flowers. The straight stems will conceal the curved ones. Tuck a few pieces of foliage upright in any empty looking spots and tie a piece of thread around the stems to mark the position of the ribbon. Cut a generous length of ribbon and tie it in a relaxed, floppy bow to cover the thread.

Tall and elegant, these salmon-coloured rose heads sit proudly aloft their dense green leaves in a natural twig basket. Planting them in rows like this creates interesting straight lines and sharp angles, not usually associated with flowers. Here, the straight stems are echoed by the vertical lines of the basket. The whole effect is softened by gauzy ribbon which also complements the lovely colours of the blooms.

Rich, ruby red 'Mercedes' roses and the natural shades of sea lavender (*Limonium tataricum*) create this luxurious and romantic tree.

The trunk is made up of three branches encrusted with lichen. Around this I have wound a writhing length of burr to create interest and movement.

All topiary trees such as this are made in the same way. You will need a container, some plaster of Paris, newspaper and a plastic bag to begin. Your trunk can be found on any woodland walk or from the prunings of your own garden. However, trunks are deceptively long, so measure yours out against the container first.

Line the container with a little crumpled newspaper, then open out the plastic bag to accommodate the plaster. Mix the plaster of Paris according to the instructions on the packet and half fill the plastic bag. Take your pre-measured trunk and plunge it into the plaster, spooning the remaining mixture around the trunk base. Leave this to dry, checking it periodically, so that the trunk does not lean over too much.

My plaster took only ten minutes to become firm, but I then left it overnight to dry out completely.

Some plaster expands on drying, so the crumpled newspaper will accommodate this.

For the next step, you will need a large sphere of floral foam and glue gun. Push the foam down hard on to the trunk, gouging out some of the foam to allow a hollow for the trunk. When you are happy with the positioning, glue the foam on to the trunk, pushing it down firmly until the arrangement feels secure, as the foam will be taking the weight of the display.

Taking your roses and sea lavender, begin by measuring out the height of the first stem at the top of the sphere. All the other pieces will need to be planted to this same height to give the tree a round appearance. So, with a pair of sharp scissors, begin trimming and planting a section at a time. Push the stems straight into the foam to prevent them crossing.

Occasionally, step back to assess your progress. If you notice an empty space, gently ease a flower in the gap to fill it.

Once the mop head is complete, finish off the base by packing bun moss (*Grimmia pulvinata*) up around the trunk.

This topiary tree uses one of the most abundant ingredients: sea lavender. Readily available and inexpensive, the sea lavender creates a lacy, white background for the glorious rich, red roses. Make the trunk of the tree more interesting by twisting a burr, bramble or vine around it before setting it into the base.

Line the container with crumpled paper and a plastic bag. Half fill the bag with plaster of Paris and insert the trunk. Top up the plaster and leave to dry.

Push the foam on to the trunk to make an impression. Gouge out a little of the foam to make a hole. Glue the trunk into the hole, pushing the two firmly together.

Pastel tree

Warm peach and pastel greens combine beautifully in the mop head of this tree. To achieve the best balance, use more of one ingredient than the other, even if the ratio is small. Here, there are slightly more poppy heads than roses. For an extra feature which gives additional interest, create a small frill of another ingredient at the bottom of the mop head. I have tucked in dyed sea lavender.

Choose pretty pastel shades of peach and the palest green or similar colours to complement your soft furnishings. I made this arrangement for a dinner party, so placed sweetie biscuits around the trunk for delicious after-dinner nibbling.

This tree is made in the same way as the Sweetheart Tree but, as the mophead is busier, it uses a short simple trunk.

The mop head is made from 'Gerdo' roses and poppy (*Papaver*) seedheads and, like the previous tree, built up in sections. Do not strip off all the foliage from the roses as it helps to fill in any gaps.

Finish the Pastel tree with the smallest amount of peach-dyed sea lavender (*Limonium tataricum*) inserted underneath the tree to form a little frilly petticoat.

Egg tree

Eggs really interest me. Their fascinating ovoid shape and differing hues of pale pinky yellows, warm beiges and bronzed skin tones offer unusual potential.

I made up the base and trunk as for the Sweetheart Tree, but here I used a larger foam sphere.

There are 92 hens' eggs in this arrangement and, as each one has to be blown, my daughters soon tired of omelettes and soufflés.

I discovered the most convenient way to make any arrangement involving large numbers of eggs was to build them up gradually. Blowing one or two eggs is one thing, blowing 92 is quite another!

Striking, fascinating and sensual, this extraordinary topiary tree is made from ordinary hens' eggs. Each egg must be blown and wired, with the addition of a pretty glass bead, before it can be set into the mop head. Violet and peach colours work well with the natural colours of eggs; I have used violet reindeer moss in the base and pale peach as a background colour for the foam.

The easiest way to blow an egg is to take a large needle or hat pin and push it through the length of the egg. Gently ease away a little egg shell from the pin prick at the blunt end of the egg and blow from the pointed end.

After a few attempts you will soon become as practised as me.

Once you have assembled your eggs and basic tree, you will need to gather together some beige or pale peach emulsion paint, medium gauge stub wire, pretty glass beads, reindeer moss and an Easter chick or two.

As gaps on this arrangement will be unavoidable, paint the foam sphere first in a pale flesh colour. Once it is dry you can begin.

Take a 20cm (8in) length of stub wire and thread the first 3cm (1¼in) through your bead. Double the wire back on itself

and twist the two ends together right up to the bead.

Now thread the beaded wire from the pointed end of the egg through to the blunt end. You will be left with a wire 'tail'. Bend this 'tail' back on itself to double it, so that when you push the wired egg into the foam sphere, the wire will not buckle.

Taking the wired eggs, start at the top of the tree, as usual, and progress down the sides, nestling one egg up against another.

For the base of the tree, I disguised the plaster with light violet-coloured reindeer moss and added two chicks and a few painted eggs.

I adore this little folly, but even if you are not enamoured with it, it does demonstrate the interesting use of eggs in floral arrangements.

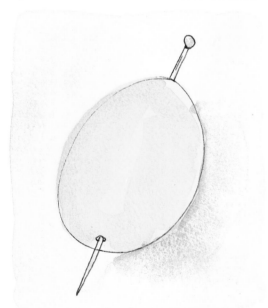

Push a hat pin or large needle through the length of the egg. Then gently ease away a little shell from the blunt end by wiggling the needle. Blow from the pointed end and the contents will empty out of the larger hole at the blunt end.

Thread 3cm of 20cm long stub wire through a bead. Bring the wire back on itself and twist the two ends together right up to the bead. Now thread the beaded wire from the pointed end of the egg through to the blunt end.

Teasel tree

This little tree is made with the fruits of a seashore blustery walk with my young daughters. Had we not been gathering, we would not have walked so long or so far.

The basic tree is made just like the others, using just one rather short, thick trunk and a large cone of floral foam. It is planted in an ordinary, weathered flowerpot.

To decorate the basic tree you will need to gather teasels (*Dipsacus sativus*) of all differing sizes.

These are mixed with soft rush (*Juncus effusus*) which grows in wet and marshy ground. Despite its name, soft rush has a hard, dark dried seedpod with a vicious spike and spears of leaves which look most attractive darting out from the outline of this display.

Musk thistles (*Carduus nutana*) and a natural jute ribbon complete this arrangement.

Sort the teasels into large and small sizes. You will need the smaller ones for the top and the largest ones for the base of the tree to give it visual weight.

Begin at the top of the tree, inserting a teasel, then progress down the cone, planting the teasels dispersed with rush to fill in the gaps.

Underneath the cone, plant a soft rush petticoat.

Fill around the base of the pot with musk thistles or you could use husks of spent beech nuts (*Fagus sylvatica*) or even crumbled bark.

Finally, take the soft rush leaves and place them strategically throughout the display. Tie a jute ribbon around the base as a soft contrast.

This natural-style Teasel tree – with its dusky browns and rich earth colours – is in complete contrast to the other topiary trees.

WREATHS & GARLANDS

The traditional woven wreath is centuries old. Representing the perpetual renewing of the seasons, the wreath is used for tribute, memorial and celebration and it is another means of displaying nature's fruits within the home.

The selection of wreaths in this chapter offer some ideas with which you can experiment. Create your own Celebration garland, whether using summer flowers, grasses, pine cones or different media such as feathers or shells.

Two basic methods are used to create these wreaths: the Celebration, Summer and Herb wreaths are constructed using a floral foam circle. The Autumn wreath is very easily achieved by twisting natural materials together.

Summer splendour garland

Combine bright, vibrant purples and pinks to make a summer's garland.

This design is worked on a floral foam circle, in the same way as the Celebration Garland and Herb Wreath, but the choice of materials gives an entirely different effect to hang on your wall or door.

The success of this garland depends on grouping the elements together so that they retain their individual character. Try to avoid 'scattering' ingredients, as the end result will be a rather messy blur.

The principal flowers are roses, hydrangea and deep lilac statice (*Limonium sinuatum*). To these rather rounded forms, I added bunches of barley (*Hordeum*) and fluffy hare's tail grass (*Lagurus ovatus*) to give length and movement. For contrasting texture I selected two slightly exotic ingredients: rattan palm (*Calamus*) and white-tipped cones. For depth and infill, I used spiral eucalyptus leaves (*Eucalyptus pulverulenta*) and scraps of rose foliage.

A large paper bow was the only other element.

Paper ribbon is a wonderful complement to dried flowers, reflecting their more subtle tones and hues. It can be bought from stationers or florists in tightly coiled lengths. Simple rub the coil between your thumbs and fingers to unravel it to its full width, then treat it in the same way you would fabric ribbon.

The other advantage to paper ribbon is that it holds its shape well when tied into a bow.

It is with the ribbon that I began my garland. As the bow is so full, I tied this first around the foam circle.

I then began folding my barley in half to give me both ears and stalks together and secured two hearty clusters with sticky tape. I pushed one cluster into the foam beneath the bow.

Many people associate wreaths and garlands with winter decorations. This display is a tribute to summer with its pretty pinks and purples and the rich clusters of roses. The wonderful blue-green bow is made from paper ribbon; it is the perfect complement to the eucalyptus, hydrangea and rose leaves. Clusters of wheat and fluffy hare's tail grass give movement to an otherwise static arrangement.

Vibrant purple statice sits next to cerise pink roses. This garland works well because each ingredient is set into the circle in groups. For ease, gather each cluster and bind it with sticky tape before inserting it into the foam. This gives a much better effect than if you try to insert the ingredients individually.

Fold three or four stems of barley or wheat in half to give you both stalks and ears together. Bind the fold with sticky tape before pushing it into the foam.

Underneath the barley I inserted one hydrangea head. Take care with hydrangeas as the tiny florets easily break off. If you buy hydrangea heads, they are usually wired with stub wire. This makes them stronger and easier to insert into the foam. However, if you take care, you can push them in by their own stems.

Behind this, at the edge of the garland, push in a few sprays of rose leaves.

Continue working around the garland in a clockwise direction. Tuck a little statice next to the hydrangea, then insert three or four deep crimson roses.

Push in a large cluster of rattan palm just above and beyond the roses. The cones sit below this, and these will need wiring before inserting them into the foam. (Full instructions for wiring cones appear on page 115.)

Continue around with a clump of hare's

tail grass; bunch this together and bind with sticky tape before inserting it in to the foam. Next, tuck in more statice and another cluster of barley. In amongst this, gently push in three, bright red roses.

As you work, continue to assess your progress for weight, density, colour and texture combinations.

Where there are gaps, tuck in small sprays of rose leaves. These are excellent for infill, adding a contrast of texture and colour.

Form another two bunches of fluffy hare's tail grass and insert them close to each other at the next section. In amongst this nestle a pink rose.

Come up the side of the garland with a profusion of eucalyptus and rose leaves. Among this mass of bluey-greens, nestle three more pink roses and, towards the top, a large cluster of statice.

Finally, work the remaining section of the garland with eight or nine smaller pink roses, inserting them so that they sweep down from the bow.

At the top, tucked in behind the bow, push another cluster of hare's tail grass and a little sprig of hydrangea.

It is often effective to add a little touch of the unusual to your displays. Here, a complete contrast of tone and texture is supplied by the bobbly rattan palm and white tipped, furry cones.

Festive table swag

Laden with summer's late glories and the heady fruits of dappled autumn days, this sumptuous floral swag boasts an abundance of nature's riches.

To create a feeling of movement, vitality and surprise, the choice of fruits and flowers – and their juxtaposition to one another – is extremely important.

Here, I have decorated a small table with a swag of materials of varying tones and textures. I have used some fairly exotic varieties, but felt that the design and occasion warranted something a little special. Good dried flower suppliers should be able to obtain the more unusual items but here is a good example where you can experiment with other materials of your choice.

Gourds and carline thistles (*Carlina acaulis*) form the focal points of the swag; quails' eggs, baby corn or maize (*Zea mays*), cocoa pods and Badam (a most interesting Indian seedpod) add contrasting texture, while Chinese lanterns (*Physalis alkekengi*) and *Protea compacta* fill in the outline. Superb heavy ribbon and gigantic tassels complete the display.

Mechanics needed for the swag include floral foam, string, wire mesh, stub wire, a glue gun, and felt. Nails and a hammer will be necessary to secure the swag to the underside of the table if you are decorating a large trestle table. However, if you are using a good piece of furniture, it is best to tightly lash around the table leg with string and sew the swag through the cloth to the string with strong thread. Although do not secure a heavy swag using this method.

Create this sumptuous swag for a special banquet or grand ball. The swollen gourds, bursting corn and the fiery Chinese lanterns create a look of abundance and opulence.

Rich colours and exotic contours are the key to this swag's success. Corn and cocoa provide length and movement, while gourds and Chinese lanterns give substance and warm hues. The quails' eggs offset all the other ingredients with their wonderful speckled shells.

To judge the length and depth of the swag, I draped a piece of string along the table and cut it when I was satisfied with the effect.

When you have established the size of our swag, lay the string on a flat work surface and take two bricks of floral foam. Place one brick in the centre of the string and cut the other brick in two, placing the pieces on either side.

Now take a piece of wire mesh and mould it around the foam, into the form of a swag. I tested this against the table, remembering that the finished swag would be generous with ingredients.

Firmly secure the wire mesh edges by intertwining them together and twisting them back into the foam.

Cut a piece of felt the size and shape of the swag and glue it to the back of the wire mesh. This will help avoid any damage to your furnishings.

Now the fun begins. Before you insert anything into the swag, you must gather all your ingredients together.

First, wire the heavy items such as the corn (maize) and gourds.

The quails' eggs will need to be blown and wired with a glass bead. Instructions to do this appear on page 114.

Once you have assembled several clusters of eggs, put them to one side. I used three dozen, nearly 40 eggs! However, these do make the most heavenly omelette.

Wire the baby maize and double wire the heaviest gourds. This will give the gourd additional security and prevent it from slipping in the wrong direction.

The best way to wire these weighty fruits, is to bore a hole through them and out the other side with a skewer. Push two pieces of stub wire through the holes, take the ends and twist them together.

If the gourds are very heavy, it is best to wire them in two places. Simply bore another two holes a little higher up the side of the fruit and insert more wire.

From the ribbon, form a rosette. This is easily done by pleating the ribbon folds one against the other. Push a wire through the folds to secure them; by twisting the ribbon slightly, the folds fall open into a rosette.

Attach the rosette to the beginning of the wire frame and wrap the ribbon around and around the swag, finishing at the other end with another rosette.

Take six giant tassels and drape three from each rosette, securing them from behind with wire pushed into the mesh frame. Pleat parts of the cord holding the tassel to give additional movement within the rosette, and trail some cord over the ribbon to enhance the interesting texture.

Having wrapped the wire frame with ribbon and cord, I then attached it against a wall to work.

Begin centrally with the gourds, tilting them against one another and tucking the open baby maize in behind them to complete a focal triangle.

Wedge an intriguing badam seedpod beneath the central point, pushing in more wired baby maize behind to serve as a background.

Work from the centre outwards, placing clusters of quails' eggs, another badam, and trails of cocoa pods flowing towards the outer edges.

In against the egg clusters tuck groups of Chinese lanterns with their brilliant orange hues and contrast the texture with straw-like carline thistles. (Be wary of exactly where you plant these, as extracting them can be painful!)

On the left hand side, I have added a group of smaller gourds to balance the display, and tucked in *Protea compacta* to help strengthen the outline.

Lastly, I wired trailing cocoa pods and added these in among the tassels.

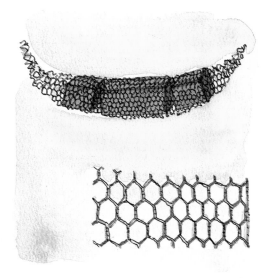

Place one brick of foam in the centre of the wire mesh. Cut another brick in half and place these on either side of the first brick. Now wrap the mesh up around the foam and mould it into a swag shape.

Use a skewer to bore a hole through the gourd in two places. Push heavy duty stub wire through the holes and twist the ends together. If the fruit is very heavy, bore another two holes and wire it twice.

When you are satisfied with the effect of the display, begin to glue the hollowed out bread into position. Now leave the bread for two or three days to become stale. Coat all the bread surfaces with varnish, adding a sprinkle of poppy seeds to some items if you wish; they easily stick to the wet varnish. Leave the complete display to dry overnight.

To complete the arrangement, gently bend stems of wheat and barley in the centre so they form a tight V shape. This way you have both stalk and ear for use; these give height and movement to an otherwise dumpy arrangement.

Now glue clumps of barley and wheat into the display. You can bind them into clusters first with a little natural raffia or sticky tape.

Add your ravishing bow of paper and your kitchen folly is complete.

Scoop out as much bread as possible through a hole in the base. This will prevent it from going mouldy.

Roses cast in bronze

The simplicity of this mound of roses set against the turquoise-green of the dish is extraordinary. The bowl itself is quite a feature, but the roses enhance its beauty.

A round piece of floral foam, a large stone and deep red roses are all that are required for this design.

Embed a stone into the floral foam to prevent the rose mound slipping about.

Now, simply insert the roses, cutting their stems short, to create a little mound or hillock in the centre of the bowl.

One of the simplest, yet most effective, displays in the book, the design does require a quantity of roses and probably more than you might think. In my design I have used a little under 40 rose heads.

This large, verdigris dish is a stunning feature in itself. Witness how it has been enhanced with a small mound of deep scarlet roses, packed into its base. This is an excellent example of a successful marriage between two simple elements.

Golden sconce

The dramatic curves of this stately sconce made it a perfect item to embellish with flowers, fruits and ribbon. I have given the whole display a sumptuous richness by spraying most of the floral material in glistening gold. The finished result is magnificent, with echoes of the baroque.

I have used the similar shapes of love-in-a-mist (*Nigella damascena*), safflower (*Carthamus tinctorius*) and poppy heads (*Papaver*) together with common wheat (*Triticum aestivum*), the long-leaved eucalyptus (*Eucalyptus kruseana*) and rich, red roses.

Floral foam, tape, gold spray paint and a rich brocade ribbon are the other elements needed here.

Begin by taping an oblong piece of foam upright to the back of the sconce.

First spray all the floral material, with the exception of the roses and foliage, gold. Leave to dry.

Next, wind your ribbon around the sconce and finish with a large rosette bow low down in the centre. (To create this type of bow, see page 49.)

Take your largest poppy heads and place these in a group in the centre, just above the rosette, to form the focal point.

Now work upwards and outwards with groups of love-in-a-mist and poppy heads grouped in threes and fives. Balance the arrangement, but it is not necessary to create symmetrical groups.

To the edges, add in clusters of safflower and wheat.

For the lower edge, use longer stems of wheat and safflower.

For depth and interest, take a few stems of your long-leaved eucalyptus and insert these around the outline.

Finally, add five deep red roses just above the centre. This offsets the whole display and brings together all the other elements in perfect harmony.

For this shape sconce you will need an oblong piece of foam. Tape the foam to the sconce using masking or florists' tape. Other types of tape do not stick so well.

Wind co-ordinating ribbon around the "branches" of the sconce and finish with a large rosette bow. Push in the largest poppy heads to form a focal point.

A plain wall sconce is beautifully decorated with gold and red. Paint-sprayed wheat and poppy heads in glistening gold form the basis of the display; richly patterned ribbon hangs in luxurious drapes, while bright scarlet roses offset the complete arrangement. Dark green foliage provides a perfect backdrop.

Autumn sheaves

Traditionally, cereal crops were gathered into sheaves at harvesting. Their beautiful shapes and forms would grace the church at harvest festivals as people gave thanks for the grain and crops gathered.

Today, these displays are once again admired for their simplicity and style.

WHEATSHEAF
A sheaf of gathered wheat is a perfect representation of nature's prosperity and, because of its classical simplicity, can look stunning in almost any setting.

However, beware! When I first made a wheatsheaf I thought it would be a very easy task to accomplish, but it can be deceptively difficult.

There is a recipe to success, although you still might encounter a few problems with your first attempt.

Take a bunch of common wheat (*Triticum aestivum*) and peel back the protective leaf which sheaths the husk.

Assemble string, a large newspaper and sharp scissors. You will also need a natural ribbon, raffia or grasses to cover the tie.

Place the broadsheet newspaper on a large work surface (I put mine on the floor). Prop up the sides of the newspaper with piles of books to form a cradle. Lay a piece of string across the paper, allowing each end of the string to drape over either side of the cradle.

Lay the wheat in the cradle, aligning the top of the wheat with the edge of the newspaper.

I used six bunches of wheat to fill my cradle.

Gather up the string and tie it loosely. Now, take your courage in both hands and, keeping the bunch exactly where it is, twist your wheatsheaf very slightly. (The second you pick up the sheaf, it goes everywhere, so do take care.)

Traditional style sheaves have become most popular; yet their simplicity belies the skill required in their construction.

Tighten the string, so that the sheaf can no longer move and trim the ends of the stalks flat.

Only now can you remove the sheaf from the newspaper and stand it up.

Cover the string with plaited raffia, a huge paper bow or twisted grasses tied in reef knots, in the secure knowledge that the string underneath is holding the arrangement in place.

The sheaf would look equally effective using lavender or barley.

HARVEST SHEAF

The vermillion colours of autumn are collected together in this glowing sheaf. Orange, green and gold jostle for position here.

I have used burnt orange safflower (*Carthamus tinctorius*) peeling out of their delicious green buds, lonas or golden ageratum (*Lonas*) and yellow, orange and salmon strawflowers (*Helichrysum bracteatum*). The whole sheaf nestles amidst a feathery halo of black-eared barley (*Hordeum*).

You will also need to hand some natural and green raffia to tie the sheaf together. Although I achieved this arrangement by myself, it might be helpful to have a friendly pair of hands assist in tying the sheaf together.

Trim all the stems so that they are the same height. Now take the safflowers, strawflowers and some of the lonas and gather these together in a bunch. Try to intersperse the colours so that there are no clumps of the same hue.

It is important to keep the stems and flower heads level, so avoid putting the sheaf down until it is finished.

Hold the sheaf in one hand and with the other slip a loop of raffia around the stems. (Another pair of willing hands could help you here).

This is the tricky part, as you want to complete the sheaf with a circle of lonas and finally a halo of barley for the outer edge.

The best way to achieve this is to keep hold of the loosely-tied bunch and insert first the lonas then the barley until the sheaf is complete.

Seen from above, the Harvest Sheaf displays its neat symmetrical lines and the halo of barley "whiskers". As this is all constructed in one hand, it demonstrates the need to keep turning the sheaf as you build it up. Different colours, for example, pale pinks, would create a more subtle variation on this theme.

Drape a large format newspaper between two piles of books to form a cradle. Lay a piece of string across the newspaper, as shown, ready to take the wheat.

Hold the sheaf in one hand and loop a piece of raffia around it. Now add in the outer layers of lonas and barley. Do not put the sheaf down until it is tied.

Now pull the raffia tightly. This action will pull the flowers into a dome shape and the stalks into a twist. Secure the sheaf with a tight knot.

To keep the sheaf in good shape, add another, thicker band of raffia, as this allows for less movement.

To trim, finish with wispy bows of green and natural raffia.

The completed display has the appearance of an impromptu bunch brought into the home from a country walk, and certainly belies the patience of achieving this effect.

MINIATURES, GIFTS & ORNAMENTS

In this chapter I have explored various ways of using miniature arrangements to decorate objects in the home and other items more traditionally associated with a floral theme: hats and hair ornaments.

There are also some clever gift ideas and ways of decorating ready-wrapped presents with leaves or tiny floral posies.

Many of these ideas use small amounts of floral material, yet are just as effective as larger displays. Of all the designs in this book, the following ideas are sure to inspire you to adapt, experiment and create your own novelties.

Miniature baskets

Charming little baskets have a special appeal. When selecting ingredients, you will find you can use lots of reject material which is too short, small or delicate for other displays.

Watch out for little baskets in florists, department stores or even toy shops. They are inexpensive and can be transformed with a minimum of materials.

Each basket needs a snug filling of floral foam before you begin.

WHEAT AND COBALT BLUE
Here, I have established an outline of common wheat (*Triticum aestivum*), filling in with the deep cobalt blue of the tops of delphinium. Tucked in are the complementary colours of poppy (*Papaver*) heads; these also add a delightful contrast of texture.

Choose some giftwrap ribbon of a complementary shade to tie around the basket and finish with a bow. Create the ringlets on the bow by drawing the blade of a pair of scissors along the ribbon ends.

SUNSHINE YELLOW BASKET
Cheerful little rhodanthe or sunrays (*Helipterum*) nestle into this tiny basket. The stalks are very fragile, but on this scale you should be able to push them carefully into the foam. If some break off you can simply glue them on to the foam. Once again, use a complementary gift ribbon to complete the display.

SHADES OF VERMILLION
The little oblong basket is filled with strawflowers (*Helichrysum bracteatum*) in shades of deep crimson and vermillion. I filled in with brown clubrush (*Scirpus*); you can use any tufted grass or reed here. Miniature poppy (*Papaver*) heads are tucked into this riot of colour. The browns and beiges perfectly complement this rustic little basket.

PEARL WHITE DISPLAY
The delicate form of bleached gypsophila or baby's breath creates the basis and outline of this elegant creamy-white display. A silver white everlasting or strawflower (*Helichrysum vestium*) forms the focal point; to add height and a shimmer of movement use bleached quaking or pearl grass (*Briza maxima*).

ROSE BUD BASKET
This mound of pale pink roses begins with an open bloom in the centre of the basket and descends to the rim, finishing with tiny buds. Insert the roses close together to create a tightly packed display.

I wrapped pale pink double satin ribbon around the handle and underneath the basket before tying it at the side with a little bow.

Sunrays are extremely fragile when dried, but they are so pretty with their cheerful little flowerheads. Here, begin with a long stemmed flower in the centre and work down the sides with two or three more flowers. As the heads are so large, you do not need many to make this display.

Several miniature baskets displayed together on a dresser or small bookshelf look most charming. Every one was quick and simple to construct and used leftover ingredients from other arrangements.
Anticlockwise from top left: *Wheat and cobalt blue, Sunshine yellow basket, Shades of vermillion, Rose bud basket, Pearl white display.*

WINTER BASKET

The warm, heady scents of dark winter nights fill this circular straw basket.

As with the summer basket, the rim is built up with small clumps of interesting ingredients. Here, I have used golden mushroom, deep flame coloured strawflowers (*Helichrysum bracteatum*), cones and hazelnuts. All the items are stuck to the basket using a glue gun.

Work around the rim a section at a time, glueing the items in small groupings. Dotting pieces here and there does not work nearly so well.

It does not really matter what you put into the pot pourri. Toning colours and interesting shapes work well, but do not forget fragrant herbs: basil, marjoram, meadowsweet, peppermint, rosemary, sage and thyme in particular. Spices are also a good source of delicious aromas: aniseed, cardamom, cinnamon sticks, cloves and vanilla pods are just a few that I use, as they are visually interesting too.

Other wonderful winter scents include eucalyptus and lemon verbena and finally do add twists of citrus peel for a sharp and contrasting essence.

This basket demonstrates a great use for broken strawflower heads. You can buy these heads very cheaply if you do not have any. Mix with coffee-coloured fungus and bobbly cones to adorn a simple, round basket. Fill with pot pourri you have made yourself from fallen petals, aromatic spices and flowerheads. Scent with a few drops of an autumnal essential oil – such as orange. These oils are sold in health or beauty shops.

Clove and rose pomanders

There is little to compare to the natural, warm-smelling aroma of orange and cloves, or the deep, sensual scent of roses. Use these pomanders to decorate your linen cupboards or wardrobe and allow their delicious scents to permeate the fabrics within.

CLOVE BALL

The clove pomanders are constructed on an orange. Use a thin skinned "navel" type fruit or Seville orange; do not use a thick skinned Jaffa orange as this makes inserting the cloves very difficult. Tangerines or satsumas are also unsuitable as they tend to be squashy and unstable.

Apart from the orange you will need cloves, string, and plenty of patience!

Tie the orange with the string like a parcel, dividing the fruit into four quarters. If you wish to use ribbon on this type of pomander, do not tie it on at this stage, as it can become stained by the fruit. Instead, wait until the orange has dried then remove the string and tie the ribbon in its place.

One at a time, insert the cloves into the orange in segment formation.

Now leave the orange to dry out. In doing so, it will shrink slightly.

Once the pomander is dry, you can begin to decorate the ties.

If you have used string or twine you can add amusing details to the ends.

Here, I have drilled holes through nutmegs and slid these, like beads, on to the ends of the string. You could of course use wooden beads for a similar effect.

I have also glued bay leaves to the base of one of these pomanders to create an "elfin hat" pattern. Or glue on small cones.

Always look carefully at these small details, as these transform the mundane into something special.

ROSE BUD POMANDER

The rose pomander is worked in the same way as the Clove Ball, except you use a dried floral foam sphere as your base.

Divide the sphere in half with a narrow satin ribbon and begin inserting the rose buds carefully into the foam. Finish with a rosette of ribbon for a feminine touch.

Perfect for the boudoir or your wardrobe.

Scent linen cupboards and wardrobes with pretty pomanders made from delicious oranges and cloves or decorate your bedroom with tiny rosebud balls. Both types of pomander require a little patience to insert the individual ingredients; but the effects are long-lasting and make perfect gifts for friends or family.

Insert the cloves into the skin of the orange one at a time. Work from top to bottom in "segments".

Little details turn these pomanders into something special. Glue on bay leaves at the base to create a little elfin hat.

Decorated hats

Fun and fanciful, a hat can adorn any plain outfit, transforming the ordinary into something memorable.

These hats are simple straw ones, economical to buy, and begging to be decorated. Here are three quick and easy ways to do this using natural raffia and a few dried flowers.

NAVY STRAW

The simplest of all designs, this hat is also the quickest to make. Natural raffia looks particularly attractive against a black or dark background, and this navy straw hat makes a perfect setting.

Wrap lengths of natural raffia around the crown of the hat and bring both ends together in a long trailing plait, finishing with a knot.

Tuck a few merry little strawflowers (*Helichrysum bracteatum*) into the raffia band, placing a couple at the end of the plait. Ensure the flowerheads stay in place by anchoring them with glue.

CHILD'S HAT WITH SAFFLOWERS

Begin by making a long plait from lengths of raffia. Secure the ends with sticky tape and glue the plait around the base of the crown.

Next, make a full raffia bow and push a piece of wire through its centre. This can then be twisted together and inserted into the plait at the back of the hat.

Do not attempt to make the plait and bow all in one, as the effect is too bulky on such a small hat.

However, for speed, you can buy natural raffia bows, ready wired, to pop into a display. These make ideal hat trims.

For economy, and especially if you use a lot of raffia in displays, you might try to buy it in bulk, as it can be rather expensive.

Brighten up plain straw hats with thick raffia bows or fat plaited ropes scattered with delicate flowerheads or bold sunflowers. Grasses or leaves can add height and movement to the crown. These ideas are easily adapted with whatever material you may have left over.

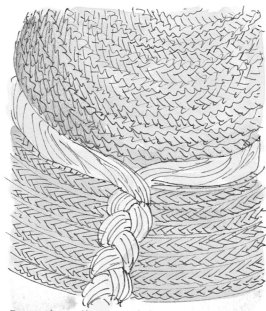

Bring the raffia around the crown of the hat. Hold the trailing lengths quite tightly and divide them into three equal amounts. Now plait together and finish with a neat knot.

Once you have secured the raffia plait and bow, work in some pretty safflower heads. These are firm enough to push into the plait but they will need a spot of glue first, to secure them.

Left: A chunky raffia bow is added separately to the thick plait around the crown. Safflowers are slotted into the plait close to the bow. **Right**: Bold and brassy sunflower heads cluster on this simple hat. Grasses are used to add a little height to the crown and width to the floral grouping.

With the raffia trim complete, you are ready to add the dried flowers. I have used just a few.

Finally, take small heads of orange safflowers (Carthamus tinctorius) and insert these into the plait close to the bow. Secure them in position with dabs of glue.

SUNFLOWER HAT

This wide brimmed hat is a perfect foil for the huge exotic heads of the sunflower (Helianthus annuus).

Sunflowers have become more popular as dried flowers in recent years and, if you grow your own, it is well worth preserving them. The best method is placing them face up in silica gel. (For more details on preserving with silica gel, see page 108.)

Glue three or four sunflower heads into place on the brim and tuck in safflower (Carthamus tinctorius) foliage to add depth. If you prefer, you can wire the sunflower heads into the hat, although hot glue should be secure enough.

Instead of a ribbon, take curving black-eared barley (Hordeum) and fold this in half so that both ears and stalks can be visible. Bind the folded barley with sticky tape and glue this to the hat. If you position these up against the crown, it gives a little height to the shallow crown of the hat.

Bunches of clubrush (Scirpus) or reed (Phragmites) are also used in a similar way, fanning out across the brim and slightly up the crown.

Creative candles

I adore candlelit dinners where you can shed the cares of the day and begin a relaxing evening. In the winter I often have a candle or two alight in the room: the effect is most therapeutic.

Here, I have combined candles with flowers to bring a touch of luxury to your sitting room or the dinner table.

Do remember to take care when using any lighted candles close to dried floral material. Most candle manufacturers recommend that the candle flame be always 5cm (2in) away from anything which could easily ignite.

WHEAT AND DELPHINIUM WREATH

Perfect for late summer evenings, over the cheese and finishing the last of the wine, this wreath is built around an iron candle holder and a floral foam circlet.

I wanted this arrangement to appear to meander between the candles, but this can be quite difficult to achieve without the whole thing looking a mess.

To overcome this, I concentrated on using the main ingredient: common wheat (*Triticum aestivum*), in clusters of threes and fives. Try to give each cluster a sense of movement, but take care how you arrange the clusters in juxtaposition to each other.

As this candle holder allowed for the wreath to sit above the table, I was able to let several clusters of wheat point downwards. This gave the whole display a sense of fluidity.

In among the wheat, I inserted small clumps of cobalt blue delphinium. Make good use of these flowers by cutting the flowered part of the stem into sections; this gives you several pieces to cluster together.

For a final touch, push narrow green and gold ribbon in among the wheat to enhance the liquidity of this display.

RUSTIC CANDLE HOLDERS

This is a clever way of using old cardboard tubes. Simply cut one down to about 7.5cm (3in) and glue cinnamon sticks all around it. Tie this with a natural raffia girdle and insert into this a few bay leaves.

Alternatively, stick bay leaves on to the base of a candle and add a green raffia band at the bottom.

Below: *Bay leaves and cinnamon sticks give ordinary candles a rustic look.* **Left**: *A stunning table centrepiece, this display of wheat and delphiniums is worked on a candelabrum. Weave some narrow ribbon through the display.*

Pretty parcels

These two playful little containers are so effective, yet quite effortless to make. Tied with raffia as a present for family or friends, they are guaranteed to bring a smile of delight.

Look out for interesting shaped containers in gift or greetings card shops, although circular and rectangular shapes work just as well.

For the star, I inverted the box over a piece of floral foam, pushing the box down into the foam to make the shape, rather as you would when cutting out pastry.

Now tie raffia, string or twisted grasses across the container to divide it into sections. Plant your areas accordingly. I have used cloves, cardamom and pale blue statice (*Limonium sinuatum*).

The round woven basket is made in the same way, although you should be able to cut your foam to fit first, in the ordinary manner. I have planted this basket with statice, love-in-a-mist (*Nigella damascena*) and *Nigella orientalis*.

Any shallow gift box or basket can be used. Section off the basket using raffia, twine or colourful string. Tie an attractive knot on top.

These charming little parcels make attractive gifts for lovers of dried flower displays. Section off small, shallow containers with raffia, twine or thin rope and plant each section with flowers, spices or seedheads. I have used the natural colours of cardamom, cloves and Nigella, with bright lilac statice for a vivid contrast.

Tools and equipment

Many people can be daunted at the prospect of flower arranging, anticipating that it is necessary to have a large collection of specialist tools to be able to achieve professional results.

While not undermining the role of the florist, spectacular arrangements can be achieved with a minimum of materials and equipment.

Certain tools of the trade are useful, however. Some, you may already have, or can improvise. Others are worth investing in. Nothing in this hobby need cost a lot of money. And once you have acquired the basic tools, you will have them forever. Other mechanics, such as wire and mesh can be used over and over again once the arrangements are past their best. Even floral foam can be re-used if the display is dismantled carefully.

With the correct materials, the art of dried flower arranging is considerably easier to attain.

I have outlined those items that I consider are useful, but this list is by no means exhaustive.

CUTTING

For cutting stems, ribbon and trimming off unwieldy pieces, it is worth acquiring some large and small pairs of **scissors**, although a pair of good **garden scissors** will service most jobs.

Dual-purpose kitchen scissors with a nick in the blades for cutting wire are even better, as these save you buying separate **wire cutters**, which are necessary for cutting wire mesh.

A light pair of **secateurs** are also useful. Keep a pair in your pocket just in case you see something interesting while out on a country walk.

I always try to prune carefully, even when confronted with the wildest abandonment. It is courteous both to nature and the next person. (Do also pay attention to local conservation orders or byelaws which prevent you from picking anything.)

When preserving with glycerine, a **sharp craft knife** or one with renewable blades will enable you to cut woody stems at a diagonal angle. This will help the plant to absorb the glycerine solution.

Floral foam is not difficult to cut, but a **long-bladed knife** such as an old kitchen knife will make this task even easier.

Most floristry books devote pages to wiring flowers and, in some cases, where the stem is too short or particularly fragile, it is necessary. However, my principal is to leave well alone unless the item is very heavy or unwieldy, as in the case of gourds, or if a flowerhead is extremely delicate.

You will find wire most useful when creating swags or wreaths, as it is a quick and easy way of making sure nothing falls off.

I use **medium gauge stub wire** for virtually everything, using two pieces together for especially heavy materials. The exception is quails' eggs. These are very fragile and need a lighter gauge.

Stub wire is sold in various lengths. It is more economical to buy the longest lengths that you can and then cut them down as you require.

Wire can also be bought on a reel. Rose wire is usually silver and very fine; reel wire is thicker and quite often black. These types of wire are used to wrap clusters of stems together or to wrap a piece of stub wire to a single stem. However, I tend to cheat with clusters of stems, using sticky tape to bind them together instead.

You can buy florists' tape – called **gutta percha** – for binding around a wired stem to disguise it. However, with the exception of traditional bouquets, it is not really necessary, as the wire disappears into the display. Alternatively, stub wire is available already coated green, should you feel any wire is likely to be visible.

Instructions for blowing and wiring eggs appear on page 114. For wiring materials such as pine cones and fragile flowerheads, see page 115. More details on wiring clusters of nuts or unusual items appear on pages 40–1.

Extra strong all-purpose adhesive works well on many displays. However, it can be messy, leaving "snail's trails" of glue all over the flowers. Much better is a **glue gun** which shoots a spot of hot glue exactly where you want it.

The glue gun is wonderful and absolutely essential. It is extremely easy to use, does not smell and the glue dries instantly.

A glue gun is relatively inexpensive to purchase and is readily available from hardware or DIY stores. I can say little more, except buy one!

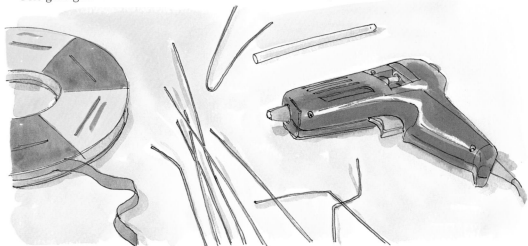

TAPE

Masking tape can be bought from art or home decorating shops, and is a useful alternative to sticky tape. It is ideal for securing foam to an awkward base, such as a candelabrum.

Do not be ashamed of using ordinary **sticky tape** for binding small bunches to be inserted into an arrangement. Items such as lavender particularly benefit from this treatment, as the least movement with these flowers, the better.

Florists' tape – gutta percha – is only needed if you wish to disguise plain, wired stems.

FLORAL FOAM

Sold in bricks, blocks, cylinders or spheres, make sure you buy the **dry-foam** specially prepared for dried flower arrangements. Dry floral foam is often grey or beige in colour and appears more "dusty" than its wet counterpart, which has a spongey consistency and is usually green. It can be cut to any size or shape using a knife.

Floral foam can be used more than once if it has not been stabbed by too many stems and is still intact.

WIRE MESH

Any arrangement which requires several pieces of foam together will benefit if held together with glue or florists' tape and then wrapped in **wire mesh**. The advantage of mesh is that it holds the foam together and helps prevent it disintegrating. It also gives a much more secure base on which to wire heavy items, like gourds or artichokes.

Fine chicken wire mesh is also used in dried flower displays when forming a swag; although you can create a lighter weight version with plaited raffia rope.

Chicken wire is most commonly sold in 30cm (1ft) wide rolls from garden stores or hardware shops. Some florists sell wire mesh in smaller quantities, often "swag-sized" amounts, in packs.

A slightly more expensive plastic-coated version is available, which is kinder to your hands and any furniture or fittings it might rub up against.

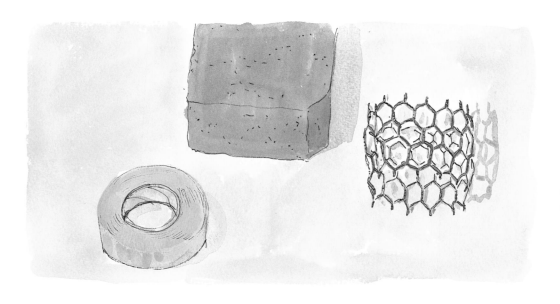

Polyurethane varnish enhances the natural sheen of leaves and other materials such as nuts and is necessary if you want to use bread in a kitchen display. It is available in either a spray or a can. Spray varnish is probably most suitable for dried displays.

All sorts of interesting effects can be achieved using **car** or **furniture paint spray**. The natural straw hues of wheat and grasses can be spray-painted to co-ordinate with your room or other elements of the display. Give lavender a richer colour by spraying it a deep blue. This looks especially good in avant-garde arrangements. Alternatively, you can spray your container; cheap plastic containers can be transformed this way.

For more information on paint spraying, see page 114.

Specialist florists suppliers may also sell paint sprays specifically designed for colouring floral foam; these are mostly pastel shades. However, you can paint foam with car or furniture paint spray.

Metallic paint sprays in gold, silver, bronze and copper are perfect for use at festive occasions. Spray some of the items to be used: all foliage looks good (it will need to be preserved first with glycerine, see page 110). Poppy heads, *Nigella*, nuts and cones are also particularly effective. Or spray the complete arrangement – container as well. Glitter can be sprinkled on before the paint dries.

Apart from spray paints, do not forget ordinary household paints. Water-based paints, like emulsion, are perfect for covering floral foam, or giving a plain terracotta pot a more interesting appearance. Emulsion or acrylic paints also dry quickly, too. However, they are not suitable for plant material.

To prevent some plant materials from disintegrating too quickly, employ some firm hold **hair spray**. It is perfect for lavender or fragile grasses which are prone to shed.

You can also buy commercial **plastic sprays** especially for preserving dried flowers from a well-stocked florist. **Artists' fixative** is another alternative.

VARNISHES, PAINTS AND FIXATIVES

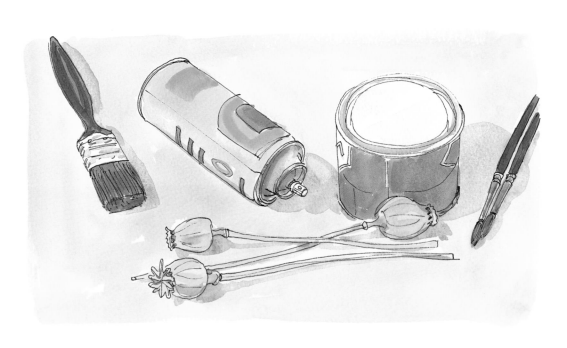

DRYING IN SILICA GEL

This method preserves the colour and form of the flower closer to its fresher state. It is more time-consuming, but the results are stunning.

You can speed this process up with the help of a microwave oven, of course. See page 109 for more details.

Geranium	Daffodil
Wallflower	Marguerite
Bells of Ireland	Sunflower
Camellia	Violet
Marigold	Roses
Carnation	Peony
Fuchsia	Cornflower
Love-in-a-mist	Delphinium
Heather	Ranunculus
Lily	Freesia
Mimosa	Hellebore
Crocus	Zinnia

PRESERVING IN GLYCERINE

This is a good method for virtually all foliage. Although it changes the colour of the leaves it makes them rich and glossy in appearance. They can also be wiped with a damp cloth, unlike other dried materials.

Chinese lanterns and gypsophila also benefit from being preserved with this method, as it prevents them becoming brittle. However, it is not recommended for most flowers.

Bay	Eucalyptus
Hawthorn	Hydrangea
Rowan	Ivy
Viburnum	Laurel
Rhododendron foliage	Magnolia
Willow	Oak
Barley	Wheat
Beech	Holly
Box	Hops
Bracken	

Construction techniques

Many books devote pages to intricate techniques such as wiring. However, I am a great believer in avoiding difficult steps where possible and, instead, tackle many things by instinct.

So here are several of the elementary principles which I employed while working with dried flowers.

With these illustrations, I have provided a series of useful references to help you construct some of the projects in this book.

Paint Spraying
This is best done out of doors or in a well ventilated room. Put the items to be sprayed on sheets of newspaper. Shake the can well and spray. When dry, turn the pieces over and spray again.

EGGS

Blowing
Push a hat pin or large needle through the length of the egg. Then gently ease away a little shell from the blunt end by wiggling the needle. Blow from the pointed end and the contents will empty out.

Wiring
Thread 3cm of 20cm long stub wire through a bead. Bring the wire back on itself and twist the two ends together right up to the bead. Now thread the beaded wire through the egg from the pointed end.

Cones

Push one end of the wire through the lowest band of scales and out the other side leaving a little wire protruding. Push this wire back round the cone and twist the two tails of wire together.

Fragile Flowers

When the stem and head is very delicate and you cannot use glue, it is worth wiring. Simply loop a piece of wire, place it close to the stem, as shown, and tape the tail of the wire to the stem.

Gourds

Any very heavy items like sweetcorn or gourds need special attention. Bore two holes in the base with a skewer. Push a piece of heavy gauge stub wire through both holes and twist the ends together.

Clusters

This is so simple. Just gather together a small group of flowers or foliage. Bind their stems together with sticky tape and they are now ready to insert – as a whole – into the arrangement.

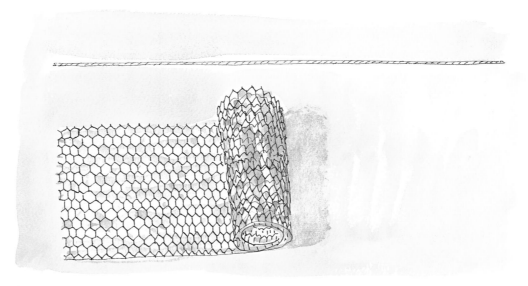

SWAGS

Determine the length and depth of your swag by using a piece of string. Drape the string along the table or shelf you are decorating. Remember that the swag will be fat with ingredients when finished, so do allow for this. When you are satisfied with the position, cut the string and lay it down on a flat work surface. You are now ready to cut a piece of chicken wire to this length.

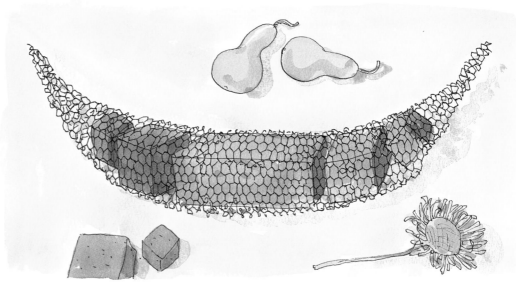

Once you have laid out the mesh, place one brick of floral foam in the centre. Take another brick of foam and cut it in two; place these pieces either side of the first brick. Now, mould the mesh around the foam into a swag shape, bringing the ends up on either side. As you work, tuck in any sharp wire mesh edges; they can so easily scratch your hands or your furniture.

TOPIARY TREES

Line a pot with crumpled paper and a plastic bag. Half fill the bag with plaster of Paris and insert the trunk. Top up the bag with more plaster and leave the tree to dry overnight.

To make the mop head, push the foam sphere on to the trunk to make an impression. Gouge out a little of the foam to make a hole. Glue the trunk into the hole, pushing the two firmly together.

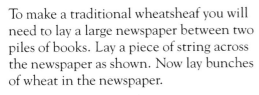

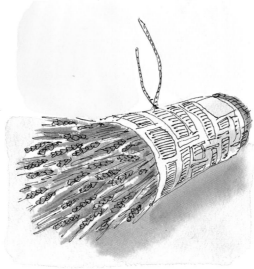

WHEAT SHEAVES

To make a traditional wheatsheaf you will need to lay a large newspaper between two piles of books. Lay a piece of string across the newspaper as shown. Now lay bunches of wheat in the newspaper.

Bring the sides of the newspaper up around the wheat and tie the string once around the bunch. Keeping the bunch where it is, twist it very slightly and tighten the string.

**TRANSPORTING
AND STORING**

Dried flowers do not like to travel so, where possible, make up your display on location. If you do have to make it in advance, make sure that everything in the display is well secured. Pack in a large carton with plenty of space and swathe dark tissue around the arrangement.

Arm yourself with your glue gun, some wire and hair spray for on the spot repairs.

For long-term storage, pack flowers in large boxes with layers of dark tissue paper gently supporting the heads. Put in a small pack of silica gel to absorb any atmospheric moisture.

CLEANING

Dust, moisture and direct sunlight are dried flowers biggest enemies. Normal household conditions (although preferably not in a bathroom or kitchen if you want the arrangement to last for very long) are ideal.

A gentle flicking action with a feather duster can remove some dust, although "spiky" items like sea lavender or strawflowers do not always take kindly to this as they can get hooked up on dusters, even with the gentlest of actions. It is probably best to use a hair dryer on a minimum, cool setting to blow away the dust.

Depending on the flowers used, a realistic life expectancy is a year to eighteen months.

Seasonal Flowers and Fruits

Gathering flowers in harmony with the environment and drying what you find, becomes an absorbing hobby.

Wherever you live there is always the possibility of collecting some materials. I live in central London with only patio tubs as my garden, yet I remain amazed at the wealth of ingredients I pick up while cycling and walking around the city.

The variety of plant life in our natural environment is increasingly threatened so, while I encourage you to forage and be aware of all that is available to you, use common sense and consideration. Make sure you do not pick anything where you are not meant to (many local laws prohibit picking or removing plant material) and that you avoid trampling any other plant life. Always use a sharp pen knife or secateurs, even when cutting grasses, as one can needlessly pull up the whole clump.

SPRING
Spring brings forth early flowers and budding twigs. On muddy walks in country lanes, look out for lichen covered fallen branches, twisted vines against tree trunks and occasionally – beneath holly and magnolia – skeleton leaves that nature has prepared for you.

In my London tubs I have azaleas, rhododendrons and camellias and they all respond well to drying in the microwave oven with the silica gel.

Bulbs are peeping through the solid earth and emerging into a multitude of colour. Although fragile, some of the delicate daffodils and narcissi can also be dried. They respond best to the microwave method.

SUMMER
Summer's abundance brings so many flowers, it is difficult to choose what one might need. All the herbs are ripe for gathering during the summer months. If you crop early, most herbs will produce again before the autumn.

Look out for the many garden flowers; the wonderful colours and textures of the peonies and delphiniums, the scents of lavender and roses.

The extensive family of grasses boasts more than two hundred species. Many of these can be dried. Also be aware of the hearty globe artichoke flower and – at the other end of the scale – the delicate gypsophila; both can be dried successfully.

As spraying is less frequent along roads, so many elegant weeds are again available for picking, hogweed (cow parsley) is charming when the seeds have formed; and look out for nipplewort and burdock.

Gather prime leaves and twigs, as this is the best time to preserve them.

AUTUMN
Autumn brings a harvest of fruits, berries, seed pods and even fungi. Many flowers can be left to dry naturally on the stem. The hydrangea is a good example, as are most seed pods.

The thistles and heathers, wheat, corn and barley, the fat gourds and sun ripened maize: all dry beautifully.

Honesty and Chinese lanterns can be found rattling in the wind. And search out wooden beech nut casings.

WINTER
Winter brings wind fallen cones, seed pods rippling in the wind, and berried holly, ivy and box.

Take out of the cupboard cinnamon sticks, nutmeg and star aniseed. Use orange, lemon and lime peel for your pot pourri.

At this time I indulge in all the florists' flowers, like the forced hybrid roses which rarely open. When they look a little droopy, I hang them on my book shelf, and prove that nothing need be wasted.

Plant Directory

As a useful reference, I have listed here all the plants I have selected while preparing the displays for this book. I have listed them alphabetically both by their Latin names and those names by which they are most commonly known; sometimes the two are the same, for example, hydrangea! However, this list is primarily to help you if you wish to seek the same ingredient. Many times, I have seen something I like, because of its shape or colour. Only later, have I had to find out what it is called, when someone asks me what it is!

Common name	Latin name
Acroclinium or rhodanthe or sunray	*Helipterum roseum*
Barley	*Hordeum sp.*
Beech foliage	*Fagus sylvatica*
Bloom broom or nipplewort	*Laspana communis*
Bun or grimmia moss	*Grimmia pulvinata*
Cape honey plant	*Protea compacta*
Carline or stemless thistle	*Carlina acaulis*
Chinese lantern	*Physalis alkekengi*
Clubrush	*Scirpus sp.*
Clubmoss	*Selaginella sp.*
Delphinium or candle larkspur	*Delphinium sp.*
English oak	*Quercus robur*
Eucalyptus leaves	*Eucalyptus kruseana*
Eucalyptus, spiral	*Eucalyptus pulverulenta*
Everlasting or strawflower	*Helichrysum sp.*
Golden ageratum or Lonas	*Lonas sp.*
Globe artichoke	*Cynara scolymus*
Guelder rose	*Viburnum opulus*
Gypsophila or Baby's breath	*Gypsophila sp.*
Hare's tail grass	*Lagurus ovatus*
Hydrangea	*Hydrangea sp.*
Lavender	*Lavandula sp.*
Leucodendron	*Leucodendron plumosum*
Lonas or golden ageratum	*Lonas sp.*
Love-in-a-mist	*Nigella damascena*
Nipplewort or bloom broom	*Laspana communis*
Peony	*Paeonia lactiflora*
Poppy seed heads	*Papaver*
Quaking grass	*Briza maxima*
Rattan palm	*Calamus sp.*
Rhodanthe or sunray or acroclinium	*Helipterum roseum*
Reed	*Phragmites sp.*
Rose	*Rosa sp.*
Safflower	*Carthamus tinctorius*
Scabious or starflower or paper moon	*Scabiosa stellata*
Sea lavender	*Limonium tataricum*
Sneezewort or	

The Pearl	*Achillea ptarmica*	everlasting	*Helichrysum sp.*
Soft rush	*Juncus effusus*	Sunflower	*Helianthus annuus*
Starflower or		Sunray or rhodanthe	
scabious or paper		or acroclinium	*Helipterum roseum*
moon	*Scabiosa stellata*	Teasel	*Dipsacus sativus*
Statice	*Limonium sinuatum*	Transformer	*Nigella orientalis*
Strawflower or		Wheat	*Triticum aestivum*

Latin name	Common name		
Achillea ptarmica	Sneezewort or The Pearl	*Hordeum sp.*	Barley
		Hydrangea sp.	Hydrangea
Briza maxima	Quaking grass	*Juncus effusus*	Soft rush
Calamus sp.	Rattan palm	*Lagurus ovatus*	Hare's tail grass
Carlina acaulis	Carline or stemless thistle	*Laspana communis*	Bloom broom or nipplewort
Carthamus tinctorius	Safflower	*Lavandula sp.*	Lavender
Cynara scolymus	Globe artichoke	*Leucodendron plumosum*	Leucodendron
Delphinium sp.	Delphinium or candle larkspur	*Limonium sinuatum*	Statice
Dipsacus sativus	Teasel	*Limonium tataricum*	Sea lavender
Eucalyptus kruseana	Eucalyptus leaves	*Lonas sp.*	Golden ageratum or lonas
Eucalyptus pulverulenta	Spiral eucalyptus	*Nigella damascena*	Love-in-a-mist
Fagus sylvatica	Beech	*Nigella orientalis*	Transformer
Grimmia pulvinata	Bun or grimmia moss	*Paeonia lactiflora*	Peony
		Papaver sp.	Poppy
Gypsophila sp.	Gypsophila or Baby's breath	*Quercus robur*	English oak
		Phragmites sp.	Reed
Helianthus annuus	Sunflower	*Rosa sp.*	Rose
Helichrysum sp.	Strawflower or everlasting	*Scabiosa stellata*	Scabious or starflower or paper moon
Helipterum roseum	Acroclinium or rhodanthe or sunray	*Triticum aestivum*	Wheat